Recove Distortted Images of God

Dale & Juanita Ryan

6 Studies for
Groups or Individuals

With Notes for Leaders

☑ *LIFE RECOVERY GUIDES*

INTERVARSITY PRESS
DOWNERS GROVE, ILLINOIS 60515

MW01076645

InterVarsity Press is the book-publishing division of InterVarsity Christian Fellowship, a student movement active on campus at hundreds of universities, colleges and schools of nursing in the United States of America, and a member movement of the International Fellowship of Evangelical Students. For information about local and regional activities, write Public Relations Dept., InterVarsity Christian Fellowship, 6400 Schroeder Rd., P.O. Box 7895, Madison, WI 53707-7895.

All Scripture quotations, unless otherwise indicated, are from the Holy Bible, New International Version. Copyright © 1973, 1978, International Bible Society. Used by permission of Zondervan Bible Publishers.

Cover illustration: Tim Nyberg

ISBN 0-8308-1152-4

Printed in the United States of America

12	11	10	9	8	7	6	5
99	98	97	96	95	94	93	92

An Invitation to Recovery

Life Recovery Guides are rooted in four basic convictions.

First, we are in need of recovery. The word *recovery* implies that something has gone wrong. Things are not as they should be. We have sinned. We have been sinned against. We are entangled, stuck, bogged down, bound and broken. We need to be healed.

Second, recovery is a commitment to change. Because of this, recovery is a demanding process and often a lengthy one. There are no quick fixes in recovery. It means facing the truth about ourselves, even when that truth is painful. It means giving up our old destructive patterns and learning new life-giving patterns. Recovery means taking responsibility for our lives. It is not easy. It is sometimes painful. And it will take time.

Third, recovery is possible. No matter how hopeless it may seem, no matter how deeply we have been wounded by life or how often we have failed, recovery is possible. Our primary basis for hope in the process of recovery is that God is able to do things which we cannot do ourselves. Recovery is possible because God has committed himself to us.

Finally, these studies are rooted in the conviction that the Bible can be a significant resource for recovery. Many people who have lived through difficult life experiences have had bits of the Bible thrown at their pain as a quick fix or a simplistic solution. As a result, many people expect the Bible to be a barrier to recovery rather than a resource. These studies are based on the belief that the Bible is not a book of quick fixes and simplistic solutions. It is, on the contrary, a practical and helpful resource for recovery.

We were deeply moved personally by these biblical texts as we worked on this series. We are convinced that the God of the Bible can bring serenity to people whose lives have become unmanageable. If you are looking for resources to help you in your recovery, we invite you to study the Bible with an open mind and heart.

Getting the Most from Life Recovery Guides

Life Recovery Guides are designed to assist you to find out for yourself what the Bible has to say about different aspects of recovery. The texts you will study will be thought-provoking, challenging, inspiring and very personal. It will become obvious that these studies are not designed merely to convince you of the truthfulness of some idea. Rather, they are designed to allow biblical truths to renew your heart and mind.

We want to encourage realistic expectations of these discussion guides. First, they are not intended to be everything-the-Bible-says about any subject. They are not intended to be a systematic presentation of biblical theology.

Second, we want to emphasize that these guides are not intended to provide a recovery program or to be a substitute for professional counseling. If you are in a counseling relationship or are involved in a support group, we pray that these studies will enrich that resource. If you are not in a counseling relationship and your recovery involves long-term issues, we encourage you to consider seeking the assistance of a mental health professional.

What these guides are designed to do is to help you study a series of biblical texts which relate to the process of recovery. Our hope is that they will allow you to discover the Good News for people who are struggling to recover.

There are six studies in each Life Recovery Guide. This should provide you with maximum flexibility in how you use these guides. Combining the guides in various ways will allow you to adapt them to your time schedule and to focus on the concerns most important to you or your group.

All of the studies in this series use a workbook format. Space is provided for writing answers to each question. This is ideal for personal study and allows group members to prepare in advance for the discussion. The guides also contain leader's notes with suggestions on how to lead a group discussion. The notes provide additional background information on certain questions, give helpful tips on group dynamics and suggest ways to deal with problems that may arise during the discussion. These features enable someone with little or no experience to lead an effective discussion.

Suggestions for Individual Study

1. As you begin each study, pray that God would bring healing and recovery to you through his Word.
2. After spending time in personal reflection, read and reread the passage to be studied.
3. Write your answers in the spaces provided or in a personal journal. Writing can bring clarity and deeper understanding of yourself and of the Bible. For the same reason, we suggest that you write out your prayers at the end of each study.
4. Use the leader's notes at the back of the guide to gain additional insight and information.
5. Share what you are learning with someone you trust. Recovery is empowered by experiences of community.

Suggestions for Group Study

Even if you have already done these studies individually, we strongly encourage you to find some way to do them with a group of other people as well. Although each person's recovery is different, everyone's recovery is empowered by the mutual support and encouragement that can only be found in a one-on-one or a group setting. Several reminders may be helpful for participants in a group study:

1. Realize that trust grows over time. If opening up in a group setting is risky, realize that you do not have to share more than what feels safe to you. However, taking risks is a necessary part of recovery. So, do participate in the discussion as much as you are able.

2. Be sensitive to the other members of the group. Listen attentively when they talk. You will learn from their insights. If you can, link what you say to the comments of others so the group stays on the topic. Also, be affirming whenever you can. This will encourage some of the more hesitant members of the group to participate.

3. Be careful not to dominate the discussion. We are sometimes so eager to share what we have learned that we do not leave opportunity for others to respond. By all means participate! But allow others to do so as well.

4. Expect God to teach you through the passage being discussed and through the other members of the group. Pray that you will have a profitable time together.

5. We recommend that groups follow a few basic guidelines, and that these guidelines be read at the beginning of each discussion session. The guidelines, which you may wish to adapt to your situation, are:

a. Anything said in the group is considered confidential and will not be discussed outside the group unless specific permission is given to do so.

b. We will provide time for each person present to talk if he or she feels comfortable doing so.

c. We will talk about ourselves and our own situations, avoiding conversation about other people.

d. We will listen attentively to each other.

e. We will be very cautious about giving advice.

f. We will pray for each other.

If you are the discussion leader, you will find additional suggestions and helpful ideas for each study in the leader's notes. These are found at the back of the guide.

Recovering from Distorted Images of God

What comes into our minds when we think about God is the most important thing about us. For this reason the gravest question before the Church is always God himself, and the most portentous fact about any man is not what he at a given time may say or do, but what he in his deep heart conceives God to be like.[1]

Most of us developed our concepts and feelings about our heavenly Father from our earthly mothers and fathers, and these feelings become intertwined and confused. But the guilty and contradictory feelings are not the voice of God. They are often the continuing voice of Mother or Dad or Brother or Sister, or something internalized that puts pressure on us.[2]

According to A. W. Tozer in the quote above, our images of God are critically important to our spiritual well-being. And in the excerpt from David Seamands which follows, we see that these images of God are formed to a large extent by experiences in our families.

None of us have perfect families. Many people have experienced parents or other family members as emotionally distant, unreliable, abusive, unrealistic in their expectations, inattentive or abandoning. As a result, we may see the God of the Bible through distorted lenses. These distortions interfere with our ability to talk honestly with God, to share our feelings with him and to trust him. Our distorted images of God keep us from fully experiencing his love.

Often our images of God influence us more powerfully than do our ideas or doctrinal statements about God because images are rooted in powerful emotional experiences. Our images of God effect both how we feel about God and how we behave in response to his Word. The process of recovery from distorted images of God involves exchanging these distorted images of God for biblically accurate images.

The displacement of distorted images of God with biblically accurate ones may not be an easy process. Tozer explains the process this way: "Our real idea of God may lie buried under the rubbish of conventional religious notions and may require an intelligent and vigorous search before it is finally unearthed and exposed for what it is. Only after an ordeal of painful self probing are we likely to discover what we actually believe about God."[3]

The following studies examine biblical texts which directly challenge common distorted images of God. Our prayer is that these studies will assist you to identify the roots of some of your distorted images and to gradually displace these distortions with biblically accurate images of God. May you experience God's healing presence as you come to see him more clearly.

May your roots sink deeply in the soil of God's love.

Dale and Juanita Ryan

[1]A. W. Tozer, *The Knowledge of the Holy* (New York: Harper & Row, 1961), p. 9.
[2]David Seamands, *Healing for Damaged Emotions* (Wheaton, Ill.: Victor Books, 1984), p. 92.
[3]Tozer, *The Knowledge of the Holy,* p. 10.

1
Distortion: The God of Impossible Expectations

Children have a tremendous need for approval from their parents. They want their parents to be pleased with them. Unfortunately some parents, often in a desire to develop the best in their child, withhold encouraging words and speak only to correct and criticize. When children are unable to win the approval of their parents, they take in negative messages, not only about themselves but also about God.

The result may be that God is seen as one who is never pleased. His standards are impossible, his expectations beyond reach. Biblical texts which speak of God's desire for service and obedience are absorbed as justification for self-condemnation. And texts which proclaim God's unconditional love may not be absorbed at all. The image of God that is created is described vividly by David Seamands:

> God . . . is seen as a figure on top of a tall ladder. [The person] says to himself, "I'm going to climb up to God now. I'm His child, and I want to please Him, more than I want anything else." So he starts climbing, rung by rung, working so hard, until his knuckles are bleeding and his shins are bruised. Finally, he

reaches the top, only to find that his God has moved up three rungs; so he puts on his Avis button and determines to try a little harder. He climbs and struggles, but when he gets up there, his God has gone up another three rungs. . . . God is that little inner voice that always says, "That's not quite good enough."[1]

In contrast to this distorted image, the God of the Old and the New Testaments is presented as a gracious and merciful God who delights in his children and loves all that he has made. He is a God who knows and accepts our limitations far better than we do ourselves.

☐ **Personal Reflection** ———————————————————————

1. What past experiences might affect your ability to believe that God has reasonable expectations of you?

2. Imagine yourself as the parent of a little child. How will you respond to the child when he or she falls down in attempting to take his or her first steps?

How will you respond when your child is hungry?

How will you respond when watching your child play?

3. Spend a few minutes imagining that God responds to you in the way you would respond to your own child.

Describe your experience during this meditation.

☐ **Bible Study**⎯⎯⎯⎯⎯⎯⎯⎯⎯⎯⎯⎯⎯⎯⎯⎯⎯⎯⎯

Praise the LORD, O my soul;
     all my inmost being, praise his holy name.
Praise the LORD, O my soul,
     and forget not all his benefits—
Who forgives all your sins
     and heals all your diseases,
who redeems your life from the pit
     and crowns you with love and compassion,
who satisfies your desires with good things
     so that your youth is renewed like the eagle's.

The LORD works righteousness
     and justice for all the oppressed.

He made known his ways to Moses,
     his deeds to the people of Israel:
The LORD is compassionate and gracious,

slow to anger, abounding in love.
He will not always accuse,
    nor will he harbor his anger forever;
he does not treat us as our sins deserve
    or repay us according to our iniquities.
For as high as the heavens are above the earth,
    so great is his love for those who fear him;
as far as the east is from the west,
    so far has he removed our transgressions from us.
As a father has compassion on his children,
    so the LORD has compassion on those who fear him;
for he knows how we are formed,
    he remembers that we are dust. (Psalm 103:1-14)

---

1. What insights did you gain during your time of personal reflection?

2. How are the actions that God takes on our behalf described?

3. What is revealed in this text about God's character?

4. Which of God's qualities or actions described by this text are especially meaningful to you? Why?

5. What is said in this text about God's expectations of us?

6. How does the image of the God of realistic expectations compare or contrast with your understanding of God?

7. How does this biblical image of God help you to feel more accepted and loved?

8. What practical steps can you take this week to remember that God is the Lord of Compassion?

☐ **Prayer** ————————————————————————

What do you want to say to the God of realistic expectations today?

---

[1]Seamands, *Healing,* p. 16.

2
Distortion:
The Emotionally
Distant God

Every family is responsible to provide for the physical and emotional
needs of family members. Many families successfully provide for
physical needs, but fail to provide for emotional needs.

Children are very emotional people. Infants experience sorrow and
joy, and they express these emotions freely. As they move out of
infancy, children continue to need to have their feelings acknowl-
edged and responded to. They need to know that their sadness and
happiness matters to the people who are most important to them.

It is not uncommon, however, for parents to discount or minimize
the feelings which their children express. Rather than providing
emotional closeness by hearing and validating their children's emotional experiences, parents often distance themselves from their children emotionally.

Common family messages that minimize the emotional experiences of childhood include: "Big boys don't cry. It's just your feelings
that got hurt. Don't come out of your room until you have a smile
on your face. Don't be silly; there is nothing to be afraid of." These
messages create shame in the child for feeling these things and

result in an emotional distance between the child and the parents.

As a result of the emotional distance they experienced as children, many people develop an image of God as unsympathetic and emotionally distant. God is seen as cold and unapproachable. He is seen as being interested only in facts and in performance. People who have experienced emotional distance in their families may ask: "How could God understand my problem? Does he even care about what I feel?"

The image of the emotionally distant God is dramatically different from the biblical image of Christ, who is called *Immanuel* which means "God with us." God came and lived with us, as one of us. He felt our temptations and struggles and feelings. He offers an intimacy with himself which includes the emotional closeness for which we long.

☐ **Personal Reflection** _____

1. What experiences in your life may have affected your ability to see God as sympathetic and approachable?

2. What did you conclude about yourself from those experiences?

3. Think about a relationship in which you have experienced emotional closeness. What are the benefits to you of having someone know and care about you emotionally?

☐ Bible Study———————————————————

Therefore, since we have a great high priest who has gone through the heavens, Jesus the Son of God, let us hold firmly to the faith we profess. For we do not have a high priest who is unable to sympathize with our weaknesses, but we have one who has been tempted in every way, just as we are—yet was without sin. Let us then approach the throne of grace with confidence, so that we may receive mercy and find grace to help us in our time of need. (Hebrews 4:14-16)

1.What insights did you gain during your time of personal reflection?

2. A high priest stood before God on behalf of the people. According to this passage, what qualifications does Jesus have to serve in this capacity?

3. What does it mean that Jesus can "sympathize with our weaknesses"?

4. How does the image of the God who sympathizes with your weakness compare or contrast with your image of God's emotional involvement with you?

5. According to this passage, what is now possible for us with Jesus as our high priest?

6. What encourages you about this invitation to approach the God who sympathizes with your weaknesses?

7. Spend a few quiet minutes before God. Picture yourself approaching him confidently. Picture him sharing your feelings. Listen as he says to you, "Receive my mercy. Here is grace for you in your time of need."

Describe your experience during this meditation.

8. What difference would it make to you as you face your current struggles to know that God cares about you emotionally?

☐ **Prayer** ——————————————————————————

What are you experiencing at this time that you would like to share with the God who sympathizes with your weaknesses?

3
Distortion: The Disinterested God

"I just wish my parents would give me some attention! I feel so alone."
These were the words of a fourteen-year-old girl who had been admitted to the hospital after a suicide attempt. She was angry and lonely and ready to give up on life because her parents did not seem to be interested in her.

Parents are busy people. Their lives are full of anxieties about work, money and relationships. They work long hours. They are tired. Sometimes they are depressed. Some have learned from their own childhood not to talk and not to feel. So they may not be very good at helping their children talk and feel. As a result, parents often communicate a lack of interest in their children. If they do manage to show interest in their child's performance in athletics or in academics, they often fail to communicate interest in the child as a person.

Children who experience their parents as disinterested often view God as disinterested as well. God may seem to be too busy with other matters to care or to listen. As a result, it may be very difficult for them to imagine that God could be interested in their daily struggles.

The God of the Bible, however, is presented as being intimately involved with us. He is interested in what we need and think and feel and do. He pays attention to us.

□ **Personal Reflection** ——————————————————————————

1. What past experiences might affect your ability to see God as lovingly attentive to you?

2. One way of challenging our distorted images of God is to meditate on Scripture. Several biblical images which picture God as interested and attentive are listed below along with a Scripture passage. Choose one of these images and write a brief prayer to God which focuses on your response to that image.

    a. Counselor (Isaiah 9:6)

    b. God with Us (Matthew 1:23)

    c. Helper (Hebrews 13:6)

    d. Spouse (Hosea 2:16)

    e. Mother Eagle (Deuteronomy 32:10-11)

☐ Bible Study

O LORD, you have searched me and you know me.
You know when I sit and when I rise;
    you perceive my thoughts from afar.
You discern my going out and my lying down;
    you are familiar with all my ways.
Before a word is on my tongue
    you know it completely, O LORD.

If I rise on the wings of the dawn,
    if I settle on the far side of the sea,
even there your hand will guide me,
    your right hand will hold me fast.

For you created my inmost being;
    you knit me together in my mother's womb.
I praise you because I am fearfully and wonderfully made;
    your works are wonderful,
    I know that full well.
My frame was not hidden from you
    when I was made in the secret place.
When I was woven together in the depths of the earth,
    your eyes saw my unformed body.
All the days ordained for me
    were written in your book
    before one of them came to be.

How precious to me are your thoughts, O God!
    How vast is the sum of them!
Were I to count them,
    they would outnumber the grains of sand.
When I awake,
    I am still with you. (Psalm 139:1-4, 9-10, 13-18)

1. What insights did you gain during your time of personal reflection?

2. What in this prayer suggests that God is interested in and attentive to you?

3. What is the author's response to God's attentiveness?

4. The author says to God that no matter where he goes in the world, "your hand will guide me and your right hand will hold me fast."
What does this picture communicate to you?

5. How does the image of the God who is attentive which is pre-

sented in this prayer compare or contrast with your own image of God?

6. How does it affect your sense of security to know that God pays attention to you?

7. What practical things can we do to help each other join the author in seeing God's attentiveness as good news?

8. Write a brief prayer, thanking God for the loving attention he gives you.

☐ Prayer ——————————————————————

What do you need the God who is attentive to pay attention to today?

4
Distortion: The Abusive God

Children silently ask their parents every day, "Do you love me?" In order to experience the answer "Yes," children need attention, affection and guidance from their parents.

Unfortunately, many children experience abuse instead of affection, and harsh punishment instead of guidance. They hear violent words from their parents, words that convince them that they are not lovable or valuable or capable. They may also experience violent actions, actions which leave them terrified, violated, with no safe place to hide.

Experiences of verbal, physical or sexual abuse can shatter any image of a loving, gentle God. God is seen instead as easily angered and demanding. If a person doesn't feel and think and act just right, God stands ready to punish.

But the God of the Bible is not an abusive parent. He is not easily angered. He does not yell hurtful words at us or stand ready to club us. He is, rather, the Father of Compassion. He is the one who heals our brokenness. He is the one who is moved with compassion by our need, and who is ready to act on our behalf.

☐ Personal Reflection ————————————————

1. What personal experiences might affect your ability to believe that God wants to heal you rather than hurt you?

2. In order to see God as one who is gentle in his love for us, and who provides protection for us, it helps to focus on one of the many biblical pictures of him. Choose one of the following images of God from Scripture and write a prayer to God, focusing on that image.

    a. Comforter (Jeremiah 8:18)

    b. Deliverer (Psalm 18:2)

    c. Father of Compassion (2 Corinthians 1:3)

    d. Father of the Fatherless (Psalm 68:5)

    e. Refuge (Psalm 9:9)

☐ Bible Study————————————————

As Jesus and his disciples were leaving Jericho, a large crowd followed him. Two blind men were sitting by the roadside, and when they heard that Jesus was going by, they shouted, "Lord, Son of David, have mercy on us!"

The crowd rebuked them and told them to be quiet, but they shouted all the louder, "Lord, Son of David, have mercy on us!"

Jesus stopped and called them. "What do you want me to do for you?" he asked.

"Lord," they answered, "we want our sight."

Jesus had compassion on them and touched their eyes. Immediately they received their sight and followed him. (Matthew 20:29-34)

---

1. What insights did you gain during your time of personal reflection?

2. When the blind men called to Jesus for mercy, "the crowd rebuked them and told them to be quiet." What kinds of things do you think the crowd might have said to these men?

What attitudes do you think the crowd had toward them?

3. In spite of the crowd's attitude, Jesus stops. He calls to the men, asks them a question and listens to their answer. What attitude does this suggest Jesus had toward the men?

5
Distortion: The Unreliable God

Many children conclude from observing the adults in their lives that people are unreliable. Adults sometimes make promises they do not keep. Sometimes they get angry when there seems to be nothing to be angry about. Adults may be loving, attentive and kind at times and hostile, inattentive and unkind at other times. These changes may take place without explanation and without an opportunity for clarification. It can be very confusing.

Children need love to be reliable and predictable. When people they trust are unreliable, they experience both confusion and disappointment. Often they begin to believe that everything would be better if they tried harder to please their parents. Children do not, however, have the power to control the behavior of their parents. Eventually, they give up. They decide they cannot count on other people. Often, by extension, they conclude that they cannot count on God. They believe they can only count on themselves.

People who have experienced repeated disappointments with parents or other significant people can develop an image of an unreliable God. He is seen as a God who cannot be counted on. He makes promises he may not keep. He may be loving one day and unaccountably angry the next.

People who have experienced unreliable parents may ask: "How do I know God will keep his promises? How do I know he listens to me? How do I know he will answer me or help me?"

The image of an unreliable God stands in stark contrast to biblical images of God. The God of the Bible is the Faithful One, the Rock, the Fortress. He is the same, yesterday, today and forever.

☐ **Personal Reflection** ————————————————————————

1. Describe one or two experiences in your family-of-origin which could have led you to conclude that people were either reliable or unreliable.

2. What feelings do you have as you recall these events?

3. Think of a person whom you see as reliable. Describe the person and your response to his or her reliability.

☐ Bible Study————————————————————

The LORD is gracious and compassionate,
    slow to anger and rich in love.
The LORD is good to all;
    he has compassion on all he has made.
All you have made will praise you, O LORD;
    your saints will extol you.
They will tell of the glory of your kingdom
    and speak of your might,
so that all men may know of your mighty acts
    and the glorious splendor of your kingdom.
Your kingdom is an everlasting kingdom,
    and your dominion endures through all generations.

The LORD is faithful to all his promises
    and loving toward all he has made.
The LORD upholds all those who fall
    and lifts up all who are bowed down.
The eyes of all look to you,
    and you give them their food at the proper time.
You open your hand
    and satisfy the desires of every living thing.

The LORD is righteous in all his ways
    and loving toward all he has made.
The LORD is near to all who call on him,
    to all who call on him in truth.
He fulfills the desires of those who fear him;
    he hears their cry and saves them.
The LORD watches over all who love him,
    but all the wicked he will destroy.

My mouth will speak in praise of the LORD.

> Let every creature praise his holy name
> for ever and ever. (Psalm 145:8-21)

---

1. What insights did you gain during your time of personal reflection?

2. What descriptive words and phrases are used about God in this prayer?

3. What phrases suggest that God is reliable?

4. What image of God comes through to you most clearly?

5. How does this compare or contrast with your image of God's reliability?

6. Why is it important for you to know that God is reliable?

7. In order to correct distorted images of God, we need to allow our imaginations to be engaged by the biblical text. Focus on the phrase "God satisfies the desires of every living thing." Picture God, the Faithful King, with his hands stretched out to you, wanting to satisfy your desires. Meditate on this image for a few minutes.

Describe your thoughts and feelings during this meditation.

8. Write a brief prayer of thanks to God for his faithfulness.

☐ **Prayer** _____

What would you like to say to the God who is reliable?

6
Distortion: The God Who Abandons

Separation. Divorce. Death. Prolonged hospitalization of a parent. Mom or Dad's endless hours at the bar. Or at work. For a child, these are experiences of abandonment. One of their parents, to whom they look for their very survival, has left them.

A child's perspective of reality is very limited. A child asks, "Why would my parent leave me?" Often the child concludes: "It must have been my fault. If I had been better or happier or nicer, my parent would not have left." It is easy to see how such a child could end up with feelings of anxiety and over-responsibility.

A child experiences terrible trauma when abandoned by a parent. It can destroy the child's sense of security. And it can leave a deep fear that other people the child loves may also leave.

Out of this insecurity and fear grows an image of God as one who also will abandon. The person may try very hard to please God, hoping that God will not leave. But the fear of abandonment by God is always there.

The god who abandons is not the God of the Bible. The biblical image is of a person who will never leave or forsake us, a God who will be with us until the end. Not only will God never leave us, but when we are lost, he will come and look for us.

☐ **Personal Reflection** ————————————————————————

1. Describe a time when you felt alone or abandoned or forgotten.

2. Imagine for a few moments that God notices that you have been forgotten, that he has been out looking for you, and that when he finds you his face is full of joy at seeing you again. Meditate on this image for a few minutes.

Describe your thoughts and feelings in response to this meditation.

☐ **Bible Study**————————————————————————————

Now the tax collectors and "sinners" were all gathering around to hear him. But the Pharisees and the teachers of the law muttered, "This man welcomes sinners and eats with them."

Then Jesus told them this parable: "Suppose one of you has a hundred sheep and loses one of them. Does he not leave the ninety-nine in the open country and go after the lost sheep until he finds it? And when he finds it, he joyfully puts it on his shoulders and goes home. Then he calls his friends and neighbors together and says, 'Rejoice with me; I have found my lost sheep.' I tell you that in the same way there will be more rejoicing in heaven over one sinner who repents than over ninety-nine righteous persons who do not need to repent." (Luke 15:1-7)

---

1. What insights did you gain during your time of personal reflection?

2. How did the tax collectors' and sinners' response to Jesus differ from that of the Pharisees and teachers of the law?

3. What is the difference between *hearing* Jesus and *muttering* about him?

4. Why do you think the Pharisees believed it was wrong to welcome sinners and to eat with them?

5. Jesus told this story in response to the Pharisees' "muttering." What does this story tell us about God?

6. How might the realization that God takes the initiative to have a relationship with you help you to be more secure in that relationship?

7. How does the image of God rejoicing when he finds you help you feel loved by him?

8. What difference would it make to you in your current struggles to remember that God will never leave you?

☐ **Prayer** ————————————————————————

What do you need today from the God who rejoices when he finds the lost?

Leader's Notes

You may be experiencing a variety of feelings as you anticipate leading a group using a Life Recovery Guide. You may feel inadequate and afraid of what will happen. If this is the case, know you are in good company. Many of the kings, prophets and apostles in the Bible felt inadequate and afraid. Many other small group leaders share the experience of fear as well.

Your willingness to lead, however, is a gift to the other group members. It might help if you tell them about your feelings and ask them to pray for you. Keep in mind that the other group members share the responsibility for the group. And realize that it is God's work to bring insight, comfort, healing and recovery to group members. Your role is simply to provide guidance for the discussion. The suggestions listed below will help you to provide that guidance.

Using the Life Recovery Guide Series

This Life Recovery Guide is one in a series of eight guides. The series was designed to be a flexible tool that can be used in various combinations by individuals and groups—such as support groups, Bible studies and Sunday-school classes. Each guide contains six studies. If all eight guides are used, they can provide a year-long curriculum series. Or if the guides are used in pairs, they can provide studies for a quarter (twelve weeks).

We want to emphasize that all of the guides in this series are designed to be useful to anyone. Each guide has a specific focus, but all are written with a general audience in mind. Additionally, the workbook format allows for personal interaction with biblical truths, making the guides adaptable to each individual's unique journey in recovery.

The four guides which all individuals and groups should find they can most easily relate to are *Recovery from Distorted Images of God, Recovery from Loss, Recovery from Bitterness* and *Recovery from Shame.* All of us need to replace our distorted images of God with biblically accurate images. All of us experience losses, disappointments and disillusionment in life, as well as loss through death or illness. We all have life experiences and relationships which lead to bitterness and which make forgiveness difficult. And we all experience shame and its debilitating consequences.

The four other guides are *Recovery from Codependency, Recovery from Family Dysfunctions, Recovery from Abuse* and *Recovery from Addictions.* Although these guides have a more specific focus, they address issues of very general concern both within the Christian community and in our culture as a whole. The biblical resources will be helpful to your recovery even if you do not share the specific concerns which these guides address.

Individuals who are working on a specific life issue and groups with a shared focus may want to begin with the guide which relates most directly to their concerns. Survivors of abuse, for example, may want to work through *Recovery from Abuse* and follow it with *Recovery from Shame.* Adult children from dysfunctional families may want to begin with *Recovery from Family Dysfunctions* and then use *Recovery from Distorted Images of God.* And those who struggle with addictive patterns may want to begin with *Recovery from Addictions* and then use *Recovery from Codependency.*

There are many other possibilities for study combinations. The short descriptions of each guide on the last page, as well as the information on the back of each guide will help you to further decide which guides will be most helpful to your recovery.

Preparing to Lead

1. Develop realistic expectations of yourself as a small group leader. Do not feel that you have to "have it all together." Rather, commit yourself to an ongoing discipline of honesty about your own needs. As you grow in honesty about your own needs, you will grow as well in your capacity for compassion, gentleness and patience with yourself and with others. As a leader, you can encourage an atmosphere of honesty by being honest about yourself.

2. Pray. Pray for yourself and your own recovery. Pray for the group members. Invite the Holy Spirit to be present as you prepare and as you meet.

3. Read the study several times.

4. Take your time to thoughtfully work through each question, writing out your answers.

5. After completing your personal study, read through the leader's notes for the study you are leading. These notes are designed to help you in several ways. First, they tell you the purpose the authors had in mind while writing the study. Take time to think through how the questions work together to accomplish that purpose. Second, the notes provide you with additional background information or comments on some of the questions. This information can be useful if people have difficulty understanding or answering a question. Third, the leader's notes can alert you to potential problems you may encounter during the study.

6. If you wish to remind yourself during the group discussion of anything mentioned in the leader's notes, make a note to yourself below that question in your study guide.

Leading the Study

1. Begin on time. You may want to open in prayer, or have a group member do so.

2. Be sure everyone has a study guide. Decide as a group if you want people to do the study on their own ahead of time. If your time

together is limited, it will be helpful for people to prepare in advance.
3. At the beginning of your first time together, explain that these studies are meant to be discussions, not lectures. Encourage the members of the group to participate. However, do not put pressure on those who may be hesitant to speak during the first few sessions. Clearly state that people do not need to share anything they do not feel safe sharing. Remind people that it will take time to trust each other.
4. Read aloud the group guidelines listed in the front of the guide. These commitments are important in creating a safe place for people to talk and trust and feel.
5. The covers of the Life Recovery Guides are designed to incorporate both symbols of the past and hope for the future. During your first meeting, allow the group to describe what they see in the cover and respond to it.
6. Read aloud the introductory paragraphs at the beginning of the discussion for the day. This will orient the group to the passage being studied.
7. The personal reflection questions are designed to help group members focus on some aspect of their experience. Hopefully, they will help group members to be more aware of the frame of reference and life experience which they bring to the study. The personal reflection section can be done prior to the group meeting or as the first part of the meeting. If the group does not prepare in advance, approximately ten minutes will be needed for individuals to consider these questions.

The personal reflection questions are not designed to be used directly for group discussion. Rather, the first question in the Bible study section is intended to give group members an opportunity to reveal what they feel safe sharing from their time of personal reflection.
8. Read the passage aloud. You may choose to do this yourself, or prior to the study you might ask someone else to read.

9. As you begin to ask the questions in the guide, keep several things in mind. First, the questions are designed to be used just as they are written. If you wish, you may simply read them aloud to the group. Or you may prefer to express them in your own words. However, unnecessary rewording of the questions is not recommended.

Second, the questions are intended to guide the group toward understanding and applying the main idea of the study. You will find the purpose of each study described in the leader's notes. You should try to understand how the study questions and the biblical text work together to lead the group in that direction.

There may be times when it is appropriate to deviate from the study guide. For example, a question may have already been answered. If so, move on to the next question. Or someone may raise an important question not covered in the guide. Take time to discuss it! The important thing is to use discretion. There may be many routes you can travel to reach the goal of the study. But the easiest route is usually the one we have suggested.

10. Don't be afraid of silence. People need time to think about the question before formulating their answers.

11. Draw out a variety of responses from the group. Ask, "Who else has some thoughts about this?" or "How did some of the rest of you respond?" until several people have given answers to the question.

12. Acknowledge all contributions. Try to be affirming whenever possible. Never reject an answer. If it seems clearly wrong to you, ask, "Which part of the text led you to that conclusion?" or "What do the rest of you think?"

13. Realize that not every answer will be addressed to you, even though this will probably happen at first. As group members become more at ease, they will begin to interact more effectively with each other. This is a sign of a healthy discussion.

14. Don't be afraid of controversy. It can be very stimulating. Differences can enrich our lives. If you don't resolve an issue completely, don't be frustrated. Move on and keep it in mind for later. A

subsequent study may resolve the problem. Or, the issue may not be resolved—not all questions have answers!

15. Stick to the passage under consideration. It should be the source for answering the questions. Discourage the group from unnecessary cross-referencing. Likewise, stick to the subject and avoid going off on tangents.

16. Periodically summarize what the group has said about the topic. This helps to draw together the various ideas mentioned and gives continuity to the study. But be careful not to use summary statements as an opportunity to give a sermon!

17. During the discussion, feel free to share your own responses. Your honesty about your own recovery can set a tone for the group to feel safe in sharing. Be careful not to dominate the time, but do allow time for your own needs as a group member.

18. Each study ends with a time for prayer. There are several ways to handle this time in a group. The person who leads each study could lead the group in a prayer or you could allow time for group participation. Remember that some members of your group may feel uncomfortable about participating in public prayer. It might be helpful to discuss this with the group during your first meeting and to reach some agreement about how to proceed.

19. Realize that trust in a group grows over time. During the first couple meetings, people will be assessing how safe they will feel in the group. Do not be discouraged if people share only superficially at first. The level of trust will grow slowly but steadily.

Listening to Emotional Pain

Life Recovery Guides are designed to take seriously the pain and struggle that is part of life. People will experience a variety of emotions during these studies. Your role as group leader is not to act as a professional counselor. Instead it is to be a friend who listens to emotional pain. Listening is a gift you can give to hurting people. For many, it is not an easy gift to give. The following suggestions can help you listen more effectively to people in emotional pain.

1. Remember that you are not responsible to take the pain away. People in helping relationships often feel that they are being asked to make the other person feel better. This is usually related to the helper's own patterns of not being comfortable with painful feelings.

2. Not only are you not responsible to take the pain away, one of the things people need most is an opportunity to face and to experience the pain in their lives. They have usually spent years denying their pain and running from it. Healing can come when we are able to face our pain in the presence of someone who cares about us. Rather than trying to take the pain away, commit yourself to listening attentively as it is expressed.

3. Realize that some group members may not feel comfortable with expressions of sadness or anger. You may want to acknowledge that such emotions are uncomfortable, but remind the group that part of recovery is to learn to feel and to allow others to feel.

4. Be very cautious about giving answers and advice. Advice and answers may make you feel better or feel competent, but they may also minimize people's problems and their painful feelings. Simple solutions rarely work, and they can easily communicate "You should be better now" or "You shouldn't really be talking about this."

5. Be sure to communicate direct affirmation any time people talk about their painful emotions. It takes courage to talk about our pain because it creates anxiety for us. It is a great gift to be trusted by those who are struggling.

The following notes refer to the questions in the Bible study portion of each study:

Study 1. Distortion: The God of Impossible Expectations. Psalm 103:1-14.
Purpose: To see that God has realistic expectations of us.
Question 2. Allow as much time as it takes to identify the many phrases which describe God's compassion for his children.

Question 3. The powerful description of God in verse 8 is a quotation from Exodus 34:6-7, where God reveals himself to Moses. "This is God's own statement in which He conveyed to man a revelation of his inmost being" (H. C. Leupold, *Exposition of Psalms* [Grand Rapids, Mich.: Baker, 1981], p. 718).

Question 4. People who have been abused or neglected may find it unbelievable that anyone would act on their behalf. Allow time for people to discuss what it means to them individually that God acts on their behalf.

Question 5. The god of impossible expectations does not understand that people have limits. But the God of the Bible recognizes that we are needy creatures. He "remembers that we are dust." The god of impossible expectations is consumed with anger when we fail to meet his expectations. The God of the Bible is "slow to anger, abounding in love." To people with needs and desires, the god of impossible expectations says, "I don't want to hear about it." The God of the Bible hears us and satisfies our "desires with good things." The god of impossible expectations is intolerant of people who are exhausted. The God of the Bible seeks to renew our strength "like eagles" (Isaiah 40:31).

Question 6. Many people think that God expects perfection. They continually hear God saying, "You can do better than that." Perfectionism, however, results eventually in both resentment toward God and a vicious self-condemnation. According to David Seamands, perfectionism is "the most disturbing emotional problem among evangelical Christians" (Seamands, *Healing,* p. 79). Healing from perfectionism is not easy. It takes a long time to internalize the unrealistic expectations that lead to perfectionism. It will take a long time to internalize God's compassion. Let this time of reflection on God's Word contribute to the healing process in your lives.

Study 2. Distortion: The Emotionally Distant God. Hebrews 4:14-16.
Purpose: To realize that God sympathizes with us.

Question 2. Unlike the original recipients of this text, the image of a "great high priest" is culturally foreign to us. The author of Hebrews tells us in 5:1 that the high priest's function was "to represent [the people] in matters related to God" and "to offer gifts and sacrifices for sins." The focus of 4:14-16 is on Jesus' access to God and on his emotional availability to us. He has "gone through the heavens." He can "sympathize with our weaknesses." He "has been tempted in every way." And he is "without sin."

Question 3. "If He merely understood the fact of our infirmities, that would be good enough. But I've got better news for you. He even understands the feeling of our infirmities—not just the cripplings, not just the weaknesses, not just the emotional hangups and the inner conflicts, but the pain that comes from them. He understands the frustration, the anxiety, the depression, the hurts, the feelings of abandonment and loneliness and isolation and rejection. He who is touched with the feeling of our infirmities experiences the whole ghastly gamut of emotions which goes along with our weaknesses and our cripplings" (Seamands, *Healing,* pp. 39-40).

Question 4. Many people find God's emotional closeness to be difficult to believe. Some find it frightening. To the extent that we feel we need to keep other people at a distance, we may also feel that it is dangerous to get too close to God. Most will, however, experience this as good news.

Question 5. This text is a clear invitation to approach. It is not an assault. It does not say, "You must approach the throne." It says, "Let us approach the throne" and lists the benefits of doing so. We can "approach the throne of grace with confidence." We can "receive mercy." We can "find grace to help us in our time of need."

Question 7. Because the healing of distorted images must take place near the core of our persons, it will require that we engage our intellects, our emotions, our wills and our imaginations. This activity is an opportunity to begin an encounter between our imaginations and the text of Scripture.

You may feel some anxiety about leading the group in this kind of activity. We urge you to trust God to meet people in the quiet moments of meditation which you provide. Read the instructions aloud slowly. Repeat the text "Receive my mercy; here is grace for you in your time of need" several times. Give people several minutes to meditate on the text. Push your tolerance for silence to its limits. Allow God the time he needs to meet the members of your group. When the time of meditation is over, give people a chance to think about what they have experienced and to share it.

Study 3. Distortion: The Disinterested God. Psalm 139:1-4, 9-10, 13-18.

Purpose: To understand that God pays attention to us.

Question 2. H. C. Leupold summarizes the message of the psalm this way: "The author is not saying that God continually puts men to the test, probes into their thinking, and thus knows what goes on in their innermost minds, true as this is. He is recording that, as far as his own experience goes, God has let the full force of His Omniscience play upon every thought and activity of the author and therefore has always known him more intimately that he knows himself. As a result there is more than a superficial acquaintance with what is being done: the Lord is "intimately acquainted with all his ways" (Leupold, *Psalms,* pp. 943-44).

Question 3. The author views God's attentiveness as good news. "The marvel of God's presence everywhere does not repel and frighten the writer. It is God's gracious presence that has impressed him" (Leupold, *Psalms,* p. 945). It is "wonderful" and "precious." God's attentiveness implies a continuing relationship. God is saying, "I am still with you."

Question 4. There is something very personal about a friend so close that he can hold your hand securely. "Metaphorically the right hand is the hand of power. This is exhibited in preferential blessing (Gen 48:14), support (Ps 18:35), victory (Ps 20:6), instruction (Ps 45:4) and deliverance (Ps 138:7)" (K. C. Hanson, "Right Hand" in *The International Standard Bible Encyclopedia* 4 [Grand Rapids, Mich.: Eerdmans, 1988], p. 191).

Question 5. "I'm watching you" may not seem like good news to everyone. What is critical is the character and intentions of the person who is paying attention. Is God watching for mistakes, or is he watching out of concern for us? Give the group an opportunity to explore what it means to be paid attention to by God. Compare and contrast this with what it means to be paid attention to in other contexts such as with family or at work.

Question 7. People who instinctively experience attentiveness as bad news have learned this fear in relationships. The fact that God's attentiveness is good news will also have to be learned in relationships. If we have critical, judgmental, skeptical attitudes toward each other, we will reinforce our fears. But we can help each other to rejoice in God's attentiveness as we learn to love each other.

Study 4. Distortion: The Abusive God. Matthew 20:29-34.
Purpose: To understand that God desires to heal us and not to harm us.

Question 2. "Rebuking" and "silencing" are common features of emotionally abusive relationships. The crowd neither respected nor valued these men. They were an embarrassment, a problem. They were in the way. In that culture, physical disabilities were commonly thought to be the consequence of moral evil. (See John 9:1-3 for Jesus' rejection of this idea.) The men's experience with rebuke and silencing will be familiar to anyone who has experienced abusive relationships.

Question 3. Notice the public drama here. Jesus is publicly attentive to people whom the crowd wants silenced. Notice also that Jesus is respectful to the men. Anyone could have seen their needs, but Jesus invites them to identify what they want from him. He is gentle and respectful in his approach to them.

Question 4. The text tells us about both Jesus' emotional responsiveness (he "had compassion") and how he expressed this emotional response (he "touched their eyes"). It might be helpful to discuss the meaning of compassion. It meant that Jesus' heart went out to them and that he was able to suffer with them.

Notice that Jesus has now moved close to the men. Earlier he "called to them." Now he is close enough to touch them. This personal, healing, compassionate, physical touch takes place in full view of the crowd. It is the central dramatic moment of this text.

Question 5. The men were healed physically. Notice also, however, that Jesus' response contributed to the process of healing the abuse which they had experienced from the crowd. After their physical healing, they "followed him;" that is, they were incorporated into the new messianic community.

Study 5. Distortion: The Unreliable God. Psalm 145:8-21.
Purpose: To appreciate God's faithfulness.

Question 3. Focus on God's faithfulness to his promises. This is a central theme of both the Old and New Testaments. Also, it might be helpful to point out that if a person is reliable, you can count on them to respond to your needs. The text uses strong images to communicate that God can be counted on to respond to our needs.

Question 4. The picture here is of God as a king who is a faithful provider for the people of his kingdom. He has "compassion on all he has made" and especially toward "all those who fall." Derek Kidner comments that verse 15 "reflects the Creator's generous joy in his world" (Derek Kidner, *Psalms 73-150,* Tyndale Old Testament Commentaries 14 [Downers Grove, Ill.: InterVarsity Press, 1975], p. 488).

Question 5. Be cautious not to communicate "there's something wrong with your image of God; therefore, there must be something wrong with you." Perfectionism and self-condemnation are characteristic by-products of dysfunctional families. Many people from dysfunctional families expect themselves to get everything right. They want their theology to be perfect, and they want their images of God to be perfect. The goal is not to "get it perfect," but to allow God to gradually change us. You cannot change your images of God by willing them to change. A deeper transformation must take place.

Question 7. Follow the pattern you used with the guided meditation for question 7 of study 2 (see leader's note). Focus on the phrase "God satisfies the desires of every living thing." Repeat it slowly several times while the group reflects in silence. When the time of mediation is over, give the group time to think about and to share what they have experienced.

Question 8. Give people three or four minutes to write out a prayer. And then allow time for those who want to read their prayers aloud.

Study 6. Distortion: The God Who Abandons. Luke 15:1-7.

Purpose: To realize that God takes initiative in seeking relationship with us.

Question 2. Just before this parable, in Luke 14:35, Jesus said, "He who has ears to hear, let him hear." The first sentence tells us that the "sinners" responded to Jesus by hearing. The Pharisees, on the other hand, responded by muttering.

Hearing implies a recognition that we have a need to hear. If you know all the answers, you can just keep talking. If you need help or wisdom, it makes sense to listen. One of the dangers of the Pharisees was that they were out of touch with their neediness. It is a common problem that in dysfunctional families people are not open to hearing. Often they keep talking about things that don't matter as a way of distracting attention from emotional pain and neediness.

Question 3. Notice also that the Pharisees' communication style, muttering, is an indirect communication, a complaining among themselves without open direct expression. This style of communication will be familiar to many from their experience in dysfunctional families.

Question 4. For the Pharisees, welcoming and sharing a meal implied an association and approval. Any kind of association with "sinners" was unacceptable to the Pharisaic mentality. This obviously meant that they did not see themselves as sinners. Likewise, they did not see themselves as needy. This kind of denial was not unknown within the early church (see, for example, Acts 10:28) and is not uncommon today. It is a way of keeping a distance from one's own neediness and from people who are publicly needy. The end result is that "sinners" were abandoned by the religious leadership.

Question 5. This text says that God wants a relationship with me, that he is aware when this relationship is threatened, that he will come looking for me until he finds me, and that when he does find me he will not be filled with reproach, but with joy!

Question 6. Presentations of what is sometimes called the "doctrine of eternal security" often miss the poignancy of God's personal commitments which can be seen in this text. God is not casually concerned about the "lost sheep." He is passionately committed to seek the lost, and he rejoices when they are found. Christian security hinges on the character of God, not merely on the technical terms of some legal transaction.

For more information about Christian resources for people in recovery and subscription information for STEPS, *the newsletter of the National Association for Christian Recovery, we invite you to write to:*

The National Association for Christian Recovery
P.O. Box 11095
Whittier, California 90603

LIFE RECOVERY GUIDES FROM INTER-VARSITY PRESS
By Dale and Juanita Ryan

Recovery from Abuse. Does the nightmare of abuse ever end? After emotional, verbal and/or physical abuse how can you develop secure relationships? Recovery is difficult but possible. This guide will help you turn to God as you put the broken pieces of your life back together again. Six studies, 64 pages, 1158-3.

Recovery from Addictions. Addictions have always been part of the human predicament. Chemicals, food, people, sex, work, spending, gambling, religious practices and more can enslave us. This guide will help you find the wholeness and restoration that God offers to those who are struggling with addictions. Six studies, 64 pages, 1155-9.

Recovery from Bitterness. Sometimes forgiveness gets blocked, stuck, restrained and entangled. We find our hearts turning toward bitterness and revenge. Our inability to forgive can make us feel like spiritual failures. This guide will help us find the strength to change bitterness into forgiveness. Six studies, 64 pages, 1154-0.

Recovery from Codependency. The fear, anger and helplessness people feel when someone they love is addicted can lead to desperate attempts to take care of, or control, the loved one. Both the addicted person's behavior and the frenzied codependent behavior progress in a destructive downward spiral of denial and blame. This guide will help you to let go of over-responsibility and entrust the people you love to God. Six studies, 64 pages, 1156-7.

Recovery from Distorted Images of God. In a world of sin and hate it is difficult for us to understand who the God of love is. These distortions interfere with our ability to express our feelings to God and to trust him. This guide helps us to identify the distortions we have and to come to a new understanding of who God is. Six studies, 64 pages, 1152-4.

Recovery from Family Dysfunctions. Dysfunctional patterns of relating learned early in life affect all of our relationships. We trust God and others less than we wish. This guide offers healing from the pain of the past and acceptance into God's family. Six studies, 64 pages, 1151-6.

Recovery from Loss. Disappointment, unmet expectations, physical or emotional illness and death are all examples of losses that occur in our lives. Working through grief does not help us to forget what we have lost, but it does help us grow in understanding, compassion and courage in the midst of loss. This guide will show you how to receive the comfort God offers. Six studies, 64 pages, 1157-5.

Recovery from Shame. Shame is a social experience. Whatever its source, shame causes people to see themselves as unloveable, unworthy and irreparable. This guide will help you to reform your self-understanding in the light of God's unconditional acceptance. Six studies, 64 pages, 1153-2.